The Dialectics of Rain

Karen Throssell
The Dialectics of Rain

For my darling Keed
and my other Kindred Spirits

The Dialectics of Rain
ISBN 978 1 76041 703 1
Copyright © text Karen Throsssell 2019
Cover design: Bry Throssell

First published 2019 by
GINNINDERRA PRESS
PO Box 3461 Port Adelaide 5015 Australia
www.ginninderrapress.com.au

Contents

The Red Witch of the West – well, of course she was…	7
Each precious drop	9
A Truffula Tree?	11
Being the Spider	13
Better Red	16
Ekphrastic Poems	
The Artist's Muse	18
Amidst the Madness	19
'*A Terre* Again'	20
Dreaming of Finland	21
Mona Poma (Fuck Art)	23
Winter's Bone	28
God Taught Me how to Swim	30
There used to be oceans	33
The Last List	36
The swimming pool – Canberra 1950s	38
The Lying Game	40
The Brown Couch	42
The Tour Guide (Cuba 2010)	44
Race – Refugees	
Honk if you love Australia	49
Lament for a bat	52
Innocent, Ordinary (13 November 2015)	54
Thinking of Home	56
Father Daughter Poems	
The Emancipation of the Empty Nest	58
Twenty-one monochords for Bry	60
A Short History of Hair (apologies to Li Po)	62
Faith, love, justice and so forth…	63

Bad luck	68
Things of Wood and Iron	71
The River Keepers	73
Mother who gave me life	75
Conversations with Katharine	81
The Majesty of Trees	83
Official Memories, Official Lies	84

Duar River Poems

Another Eden	87
If she really has to…	89
Everything is ominous	91
The Dialectics of Rain	93
Into the Wild Woods	95
Villanelle on an MRI	97

France Poems

The Dance (for Katie)	98
Petit Poulet a la Russe – a family culinary history	100
'*Le Temps Perdu*' (apologies to Proust)	103
'French country living'	109
The River Won't Keep This Friend	112
the car, the boxes	114
Easter Toll	116
PowerPoint (an informative talk to family violence workers)	117
How to untie a tie (for Rhonda)	120

The Red Witch of the West
– well, of course she was…

She lives alone in a wild green tangle
magic glade growing
in moon-washed night

> She lives *alone!*
> Who knows what she grows?
> Digitalis, wolfsbane, devils-claw…

She has a pet magpie, named Caruso
He sings in kookaburra, currawong
sometimes chainsaw

> Of course, her familiar!
> She *talks* to him, he answers
> Who knows what else they got up to?

There is brewing:
dreams and tomorrows,
wild women with books

> Mad midnight dancing, probably naked
> We know what those books were –
> Grimoires and Shadows

Like other bohemians, defying
convention, she smokes (with a holder)
wears black velvet pants

> An old woman in trousers!
> There was probably a cloak
> And look! There's the broom!

They did have their chants —*Workers Unite!*
not very different from
Never hunger, Never thirst

> So there you are!
> Confess or you'll burn!
> And remember we have your son…

Each precious drop

I dream of wanton days
lapping languid bliss
going on forever
flowing forever
time spills, flows, sinks,

spilling flowing,sinking
spilling flowing, going…gone…

Now – begrudging each precious drop
each precious drop
each
precious
drop

Making the most of small tokens
tight mean drips
tight
mean
drips

Mere damp reminders

Keeping up the rituals
Soaping small spaces
Soaping
small
spaces

The skin remembers

Echoes of water
Sad ripples in the sand
Sad ripples
in
the sand

Telling us a story:

Shower in the rain shadow
Make the most of small tokens
Keep up the rituals
Cherish each precious drop –
each
precious
drop

A Truffula Tree?

(apologies to Doctor Seuss)

Pere Charles Plumier looking for quinine
must have been startled when he first saw them.

Naturally, it had to be somewhere steamy,
monkeys swinging in a tangle of vines,

giant spiders scuttling, then a flash –
violet / magenta – a mass of tiny bells.

They could have been Plumiers,
but being a modest monk he named them

for a famous man with a memorable moniker:
Leonhart Fuchs – (so fuchsias they became).

Soon to spread from South America
crimson / lavender / orchid / indigo.

Startling colours, different but close.
Outer petals – pert like skirts or fluffed with ruffles

Doubles and flouncing triples
and always the bell, the dangling stamens

coy and lascivious at the same time, except one –
she could only be virginal

(lace curtains and lawn petticoats) *snow blush / ghost white*.
But all those bouncing frills…

Don't let the demure bell deceive you,
the original is the strumpet, swishing her skirts, flashing her legs…

'In the handkerchief code
of the gay leather subculture

a fuchsia bandana means a fetish for spanking'…
hot pink /dark purple.

My first encounter was not steamy Haiti
it could have been, it seemed so alien –

It was a Canberra quarter acre, with its tiny new trees,
bald lawns and hopeful rope fences.

A student postie, where often
for stuck housewives, my visit was an Event.

Then one magic day, my turn to be startled –
a splash of Haiti:

violet /magenta a profusion of bells,
in a tub on the veranda. Transfixed!

It looked luminous, magical, like something invented
by the good Doctor Seuss – a Truffula tree?

Who else could dream up such colours
Exquisite, unlikely, inspiring of wonder

Divine Creation?
(seashell /plum / thistle /old lace)

But not me – for me it was magic, daily magic
and perfectly down to earth.

Being the Spider

I wonder if she ever wants
to just give up?
Quivering remnants.
Again.
It's just no use.

All that intense creation.
Her whole being absorbed in
life's fragile filigree.
Then Some Oaf stumbles –
Tatters.

Just like that.
So long in the spinning.
Destroyed, in a random step.
But next moment she's at it again.
Slivers of needles, re-knitting, repairing.

Stronger than the finest of steel,
faster and faster the spinnerets flow,
then – destruction, again.
Swipe   shreds   start again
Crash   wrecked   start again.

Does she ever despair?
It's just no use.
Just want to curl up and…
But she knows if she does
she *will* die.

So she starts again –
just part of life.
Build, repair, rebuild again.
Sometimes it will last
long enough to

snare a meal, lure a mate,
maybe even have
some sticky spider fun.
Maybe even both
simultaneously.

But we're not spiders,
there is no one step back.
We build, build, grow, grow –
climbing ladders not water spouts.
School, job, money, house.

School, job, money, house,
bar, deck, pool, spa.
Upward, forward, onward.
Children don't die, houses don't burn.
And we don't just shrug and start again.

Our houses hold lifetimes,
shadows and memories
or glowing tomorrows.
We can't just shrug and start again.

But depends if we're Job
and like the spider we're stoic.
We sigh, start again,
just part of life,
What else can we do?

And if we're not Job
and it's just no use –
we have our black pit
in which nothing lives, not even despair.
Life's filled with absence – there's only what's gone.

*

But then there's the spinning –
re-knitting, repairing – just part of life.
She's frenzy and languor – abseiling on silk.
Her feather soft castle catches the light,
shivering crystals,

and we catch our breath, take it in deep.
This feels good, sweet air into lungs –
breathing, encouraged.
We want to do this.
Be like the spider – swing back.
Again.

Better Red

Red is bad
Stop! Danger! Blood!
Fresh blood, bright, frightening –
Every month?

Bad women, *Scarlet women*
Red light districts
'The Red Witch of the West!'
My grandma

Red as insult. *Commo –*
Better dead than red!
But the threatening hordes
Were yellow?

Finnish tea-pot – red
A present for Grandma, I saved for months
Being a good socialist
She gave it away

Red is good
Solidarity! Strength! Struggle!
Red flags triumphant, Workers United
(Stop! Danger! Blood!)

No one's ever given me a rose before
Robin my lover, said
It was red, wine-red
Blood-red

A tiny garnet earring I bought him
He wore a single earring then…
Being a good socialist he gave it away,
Gave it all away

Robins are red (very)
Bright flame breast-burning
Unless they are Eastern
And then they are yellow

Could they be both?
Red and yellow Robin
Red breast, yellow heart.
Who killed Cock Robin?

All the birds of the air
Were a cryin' and a sobbin'
When they heard he was dead
Better red, they said – better red, red, red

Ekphrastic Poems

The Artist's Muse

The Domain – Rick Amor

Ah Taurus, surveying your domain:
your distant stream, your rolling 'English' hills
that rusty slash of desert memory.

Big, black, implacable.
your fat back turned, contemptuous –
This bald man with his easel

does not phase you.
If anything, *he* should feel worried.
Despite his harmless green, frothy blossom,

we know he's obsessed by 'threat':
frail fence, dusty ancient hills – decadent somehow.
Sky and bull looming.

Amidst the Madness

Thinking of Iraq – pottery by Judy Trembath

Why are they always tear-shaped?
These weapons – bombs, rockets, missiles – man things:
elongated ovoids with evil points, almost phallic.
But they are not weapons, they're pitchers,
and they don't have points.
They have holes, for liquid.
They are comforting – life goes on, in the blood and dust.
Water fetched for drinking, cooking, washing.
Life-giving things – woman things.

And don't forget their beauty –
the glowing colour, their perfect tear shape.
Beauty survives amidst the madness.

'*A Terre* Again'

War and Peace – Rosalie Cogan, textile collage (black and white)

I have my medals? – Disks for my eyes*
Black binding me to black –
Lives, homes, the very earth
No gunmetal mementoes for me
Just the blood-flower of Flanders
Crying – Remember

My Glorious Ribbons? – Ripped from my back*
Bandaged in the colour of clean
A blank canvas. Start again –
Veils, sheets, a chink of dawn
And the small brave flutter of a flag
Crying – Peace!

* After Wilfred Owen

Dreaming of Finland

Finlandia, Sibelius – Aleksai Gallen-Kallala, paintings

Sibelius sings those wild white plains,
(violin's ponderous sweeps)
gleaming grey lakes
leaching colour from icy skies.
Violins scurry with an overlay
of plaintive oboe, and we see
sleds, sleet-whipped.

Dark forests loom over
squat gingerbread houses.
Carved wooden shutters –
hearts and diamonds,
unlikely ornament in such bleak space.

The music tells of tragedy, hardship
(all that slow D minor)
Large dour men
with great gnarled hands.
Mothers beseeching,
as sons leave to fight, hunt, escape –
full of stern resolve.

That harsh world had harsh gods
(The violins start to shriek –
threatening thud of bass.)
Wild old men, flowing white manes.
Waist-length beards
their only concession to extreme age.

They still pursue pubescent girls –
naked, vulnerable, their small
plaits tied with ribbon.
One, Aino, jumps into a stream, rather
than be doomed to a grandfather-husband
(even if he is a bard, and famous…)
The stream takes pity,
(violins, soft, wistful now)
she flashes her scales, and swims free.

Old women fare even worse.
Look at this one, Louhi:
half wizened crone, drooping dugs,
half eagle – talons outstretched.
Tied to a post and surrounded
by huge men with pikes and mad eyes,
who still look scared.
(violins quivering in suspense)

Sibelius's violins would wail more now –
the green swathes of giant fir
have almost gone. Not for humble dwellings,
but gifted to rapacious gods
who chew up forests
and spit out paper,
turning silver lakes brown and filling the air
with the foul breath of demons.
(Violins sob – Finland, my Finland…)

Mona Poma (Fuck Art)

Museum of Old and New Art, Tasmania, 2014

Strange man with pretend money stolen from stealers builds reverse castle tunnelling not towering.

Rips money off casinos (nerd-boy gee-whiz cleverness) builds the peoples' fun palace/temple to 'not-art'/ 'everything is art.'

Castle as art (some say best bit) perched on yellow island with moat, tennis court /drawbridge facing little boxes on misty hillside.

Sense of the benign (free art for the workers, save the Tassie economy) contrasts with slight air of menace, depravity:

And not just porno ceilings and chocolate suicide bomber intestines, the very walls:
huge hunks of excavated sandstone, echoes of convict axe, blood sweat ghosts of giant gums falling slow motion resounding boom/ crash/ shudder. Hundreds of grand years gone.

No, that's all bloody history. Just a faint echo. All this death and destruction:
…a faint echo.
So, the museum for   the UTube generation:
click-whirr rattle domino   computer   walls
flashing lights mechanical arms   hold apples
shit   machines digest   them   euthanasia
machines   for pretending to die   sentiment
machines   (drawers say I love you)   just
because   it is what you say
just   gee-whiz   techno   cleverness ?

                              But   such   cleverness...
                              Inside the boring   drawers
                              were   small   poetic gems
                              real   love   messages

We want fast and slick and now and   allatonce
allthetime   nothing shocks   but we still try
birth, sex, death   what haven't we seen before:

Large patchwork (roses and small birds) stuffed
doll face twisted in pain   torture still shocks.
No, just giving birth   a man made this   all that
fat messy female ugliness   pathetically   pretty.
Boys' horror etched into   tortured   face.

Strange brown sculpture spread over floor. Con
torted face surrounded by bubbles of   shit?
The title said *Entrails of Suicide Bomber   Cast
in Chocolate.*

I was shocked.

And is my   mind more bent than that   of
another artist? Fancy seeing   a   close-up
VAGINA
when it was just
an   ice-pick   head wound.

Boys' and machines Boys and IT Boys and sex

I know there were girls there but less smartarse
less sex shock horror cleverness wonderment
more beauty strange warped but beauty   none
the less. Yes! Conforming   to   stereotypes

>   And
>   I
>   Loved
>   the
>   Neat
>   And perfect
>   Tiny
>   Genitalia
>   And the
>   Even
>   Tinier
>   Fairy bones
>
>   Always nature wins

Can art improve on
spider-spin   and the
exquisite skull of the
smallest crab?   Always nature wins
                             But there is art in the capture

What is the weirdest material I can possibly use?
Paint, canvas, stone, bronze, wood, steel, plastic…boring!
How about kitten pelt, incense ash (shipped from Chinese
Buddhist temples) spider webs, animal bones, chocolate,
videotapes knitted into severed limbs?

What can I possibly do   to shock this jaded lot?
What about a   black madonna   more Sambo than madonna
surrounded by   dicks   arses   cunts   cut from porno
magazines   variously   connecting
simulating   cherubim   and   seraphim
(SEXIST!   RACIST!   SACRILEGIOUS!)

But is that all?
Was it in fact deeply political? Was it like you Mr Walsh –
determined to confront, disgust, outrage, provoke?

Even so, I'm sorry
I was rarely disgusted – except maybe by the chocolate entrails.
But possibly even then I was more   disturbed
And the thing is

Shock is, like everything, subjective:
Where the chocolate for me was frivolous
nose-thumbing at the shocking notion
of killing yourself and others for a cause, any cause
a friend said 'beautiful'
another – 'powerful'
another – saw symbolism in chocolate/Easter/sacrifice

What would we poets do, to provoke such impassioned and
divergent thinking?

> If I surrounded this with flashing lights that pulsed
> red when you agreed, green when you didn't, and
> violet when you were bored;
> a video link on each description which when you
> pressed would reproduce the image on your retina;
> a thesaurus reference for various words so you could
> pick your own substitutes;
> a musical score so some sections could be sung
> or maybe a button to press like those birthday
> cards or a YouTube list suggesting other videos you
> may be interested in
>
> or a direction that you imagine all of this…

But could I amaze and impress by imagination and wittiness?
Move with ferocious or farcical political statements?
Delight with exquisite reference/reverence to/for nature,
Could I make you think, laugh, question, argue?
Could I make you sigh, with delight (or frustration or
boredom) at gee-whiz cleverness?
Could I shock you just a little?

> Fuck Art – let's write Pomas!

Winter's Bone

Film by Debra Granic/Ann Rosellin, 2011

Where are you Daddy? You need to come home.
Mama's gone funny and we're all alone.

We're bred tough up here, high on the howling mountain
eking existence from bone
hard dirt. Squirrel stew in icy kitchens
takes the romance out of rustic.

Breeds cold mean men, tough bitter women.
Mouths a thin line – shut tight from silence,
all that swallowed hope.
No laughter here.

'You never used to cop no shit.'
'It's different once you're married.'

Not me though, I was going to get out
finish school, get smart. Go somewhere warm and flat
where I don't end up married to a squint-eyed cousin,
churning out skinny kids, with my mouth a thin line.

That was before Daddy left
me with the kids, Mama gone sick in the head,
driven silent and staring.
Only way out –

So, I'm not much younger
than those trapped wives
with the hostile jaws and frightened eyes.
Scared as shit of their crank cookin' men:

'*I said shut up already with my mouth.*'

God, those men, all my kin. mad-eyed, bone-thin,
It's like that up here. Grim, simmering.
All they own is their guns
and their women…

Each bleak house with its rusty cooker
sad spiral of smoke, sinister, not welcoming.
It promises Great Men, leaves shakin' shells.
No laughter here.

But though they think we're outsiders lookin' in,
(we're generations of dream cookers)
we are a family. Enfolding, engulfing,
beaten into belonging. But ain't nobody beaten me yet –

Not those desperate men – cookin' up their dreams,
not their women, lost theirs long ago.
They bred me tough enough, to know
I ain't got the taste for that kind of life,

not yet.

God Taught Me how to Swim
(statement by Eva Carmichael, survivor of *Loch Ard* shipwreck)

Minton's Peacock – porcelain sculpture, Warrnambool Maritime Museum

(In 1878 the *Loch Ard* was wrecked off the infamous 'shipwreck coast' just near Warrnambool. There were only two survivors – Eva Carmichael, a passenger aged eighteen, and Tom, a cabin boy. A pottery peacock destined for the Great Melbourne Exhibition was also found perfectly intact.)

> *Today is calm smiling blue,*
> *Hard to think of those jagged teeth*
> *Lurking beneath*
> *that fog-shroud conspirator*
>
> *The notes on the Sunday School wall say*
> *'He is always watching out for you*
> *Never fear, he'll always be there'…*
> *Lies to beguile an innocent child*
>
> *Such a capricious god, loves, forgives*
> *saves, a strangely chosen few –*
> *as on this day. He chose two from fifty-four*
> *and a china peacock*

But God, why Eva and Tom?
She who rocked and tossed five hours
clinging to her spar, then you taught her to swim.
Probably saved by her parachute

of lace and calico (having shed her
boots) and the fact that she wasn't on deck
to be crushed by the splintering mast. And why
the cabin boy, clinging to his upturned lifeboat?

Why not teach the other fifty-two how to swim,
or throw out a few more rescuing planks?
Then again, you could have lifted the fog, calmed the sea
helped Captain Gibbs sight the Otway Lighthouse.

Heartless really, of Eva to thank you
for saving her, the boy, and the painted peacock.
But maybe she couldn't understand either
why they all had to die – those brawny seafaring men

who understood their briny mistress and her moods,
knew to dive clear, swim fast away
or to dive deep down under.
And yes, they could swim, they didn't need teaching.

Was it their rum-drinking tar-scraping
godless ways that doomed them? she wonders,
kneeling in her whitewashed church
on the hill every Sunday.

And Tom – too young for getting
up to no good, destined for heroism:
trying to save the one intact lifeboat
and then rescuing Eva from the wild

surge of sea, rushing back into it
after feeling the thank-the-lord solid sand beneath his feet,
wrestling sodden corsets and petticoats
hysterical woman flailing and thrashing drowning him with her.

And dear God, why that useless bauble?
Was the peacock more precious than the
god-fearing passengers hurled into deep blue hell?
(Of course, it is now worth four million…)

Here it is still, in its sea-coloured splendour –
a tribute to Minton's hard working potters.
Looking no different after so many years
Captured forever in its dark mausoleum

Rotating slowly under bullet-proof glass
Mocking, triumphant, how could it survive?
Turning, gloating – flaunting your miracle
whilst those drowned fifty-two are nothing but salt.

Maybe you wanted a permanent tribute,
something more than our fleeting pause.
Or maybe it was your divine sense of irony –
peacocks bring bad luck.

There used to be oceans

I meant to watch the Transit
Everyone was going to
It won't happen again for 105 years
So for that reason alone
One shouldn't miss it
Such a momentous event

But it was bad timing
Trying to cook breakfast
Looking for the internet site
Didn't get the proper glasses
Then the cat was sick
Had to leave in a rush
And the vet wasn't there

In the car park I thought of Wolfe Creek Crater
Half an hour's stumble straight down
Scrubby grey saltbush scratching your legs
Looking up from the bottom of a vast hole
Past layers of centuries-stacked stone
You – a tiny blip under the sky's vast arc

If churches' soaring ceilings are designed
To make you feel insignificant,
they have nothing on this –
Looking up and into the huge blue
Trying to get your head around
The notion of 'light years'

But as I paid the vet and bundled the old cat into the car
I felt this niggle – huge things were happening up there
Whilst I performed my small chores
I imagined something like *Melancholia* –
The sinister pockmarked planet, looming to music
Inexorably bent on its collision course with Earth…

Our little transit, such an anticlimax –
A small black dot on the in-your-face ball
A mole, a blot, a sun spot
Travelling so slowly it was morning tea
Before it moved – and the biscuits were stale

Venus? The mere name is a cliché
Love, beauty, 'romance', de Milo
Contrarily capable of bringing light
At each end of the day
'Evening star' and 'morning star'
Bringer of light, reprieve, extraordinary beauty

But she is no Arcadia –
'Melanoma' may be a better name than Venus
She is surrounded by sulphuric acid
There used to be oceans,
Then there was Greenhouse
They were sucked dry

As I settled the cat by the fire
With her hourly dose of milk and drugs
I looked again at the screen
At the small fly crawling across the sun's face
And thought about the passage
Of this unromantic melanoma…

Of course we are the transients
The ones passing through
In 105 years she'll be back
And we'll be long gone
Without a trace.

The Last List

a. Write list of things not done, rank in order of importance.
b. Finish poem telling daughters how much you love them.
c. Let next door's goats in with their roses, lock the gate.
d. Listen to nursing home stories – from the worst with the kero baths, to the slightly better, with the loneliness of the non kindred spirits.
e. Read through latest *Exit Bulletin*.

f. Take top ten from list of things not done, consider why.
g. Buy present for J's birthday (remember, she's sick of owls).
h. Take all netting off fruit trees, and let chooks into vegie patch.
i. Start list of words whose meaning you have forgotten.
j. Check supply of Doloxene.

k. Write list of consequences of ignoring above list and meditate on their unimportance.
l. Write list of all friends you enjoy spending time with, cross off those who aren't around, organise drinks with the others.
m. Be nice to Indian call centre people, sign up with one of them (pay in advance).
n. Stop watching the news, or maybe watch it to remind you that the future may not be worth hanging around for.
o. Search soul for possible benefits of religion.

p. Write list of achievements – be honest, no one will read it.
q. Tell daughters they're at the top of the list.
r. Let youngest eat junk food and watch commercial television.
s. Spend time closely observing fellow man/woman and calculate how many of them are the sort of caring, intelligent, imaginative and ethical human beings whom you want to share the planet with.
t. Dismiss religion – hug sister and favourite tree.

u. Light fire and destroy all early drafts of writing including lists (except this one).
v. Order champagne and wash good glasses.
w. Organise affairs, then burn all taxation and finance files. Have a champagne while you watch.
x. Add all ancient underwear and old love letters to fire.
y. Arrange pile of photos you want to be remembered by, add rest to fire.
z. Watch last sunset with sister, daughters, friends and champagne.

The swimming pool – Canberra 1950s

Stark sparkling turquoise contrasts with musty wet
corrugated concrete, soggy togs, kiddie wee, slimy thongs.

The chemical bite of bright chlorine,
mixed with sweet tropics – coconut oil, and warm burnt bodies.

Teenage mating site – Boy, dripping gangly
macho rib strutting prance on diving board.

puffing his chest and fanning his tail.
How high can you go? How much can you splash?

Girl – cooking on her crisp towel, pretends not to notice
any more than the boy notices her new green and white check

bikini with the matching shirt which ties in a knot above the navel.
Matching beach bag too – but she doesn't expect him to notice that.

She decides to show her off carefully cooked tan. Sits on the edge.
Her legs change colour under water, small bubbles around the skin.

She would love to plunge into that sparkling blue dive deep
cool swirl head full burst out huge lung full great gulps of non-chlorine air.

But she's just washed her hair and the chlorine turns it green,
the fusty chemical smell lasts for days, and she's not sure whether the bra cup

she's sewn into the bikini is actually waterproof.
So she sighs and stays there dangling her feet, occasionally looking up

at the brown show-off boy competing to make bigger and bigger splashes.
Cold water steams on hot concrete.

Then with thunk and a gasp she's drenched – water pouring over
just-washed hair, and bikini top – through to the cup…

She's about to curse the brimming boy swimming towards her
but she notices his firm tanned arms and his straight white teeth.

And she doesn't mind when he heaves himself up
shaking himself like a young pup flicking his hand through his hair like Elvis.

She tosses her slightly wet hair, hoiks up her top
which the water has sagged just a bit, and smiles.

The Lying Game

In the photo no one else
makes eye contact
but your eyes and his lock
blatant, knowing

You can still feel the lick
of sun on your taunt
of bare shoulder,
the heat trickling

between your breasts,
the smooth cold
of long-stemmed glass,
and the stomach twist

of the lying game.
Today you are one of them,
and not.
Your mouth tastes charred meat

dripping into crusty bread,
and not.
Tomorrow is on your tongue,
when there'll be just you two

in your green retreat
beneath the trees
the gum-crushed bed,
rub of stones and prick of grass,

light speckling
his monastery white skin
as you sink, deep into
sinuous rivers.

Only to resurface
with the harsh drive home,
slumped low, fumbling for an earring,
picking twigs out of your hair.

He to his wife and kids,
one two, one four,
you with your mix
of guilt and euphoria.

The man you live with
oblivious to the flush
in your cheek, the flash in your eye.
Maybe if he looked up…

This hopeless dream –
your separate lives –
so entwined
for those short, hot, hours.

The Brown Couch

Rabbit and mushrooms, he's French, a good cook
compulsory cream. And wine, then more wine

Candlelight flickers, flatters,
Soft moody music – Piaf, Brel

The next step, the post-prandial pash…
They repair to the lounge to the saggy brown couch

faded and prickly, ubiquitous stains…
It faces a wall – bachelor beige

No paintings, no flowers, not even a book
(Waiting for Ms Right to feel right at home?)

Not content with just sitting – admiring the wall
He's pulling her over to sit on his knee

It feels so absurd – she's too old for this!
But he fumbles and gropes, up the jumper, down the pants.

He's not a bad lover once they get into bed and
turn out the lights (though he wants them on)

Aged insecurities champagnely blurred
Could have been just a night full of fun

but for the prelude on that so-student couch
so adolescent, such bad memories

that post-virginal angst:
Should I like it so much? Does this make me a slut?

Will he still respect me? Does this mean it's love?
And will he still love me tomorrow?

Now none of that matters, if it ever did
She knows it's not love, it's not even lust

Just the missing of skin, and a longing for close
A friendly companion, a bit more to life

Sex incidental, at our age so fraught
Still, for him it's a must, and for her it's an ought…

The Tour Guide (Cuba 2010)

Danny is a tour guide – twenty-five years old. Born twenty-five years after the revolution.

> Ernesto was Fidel's mate – his che.

> Ordinary becomes extraordinary

To Danny he is just another great revolutionary hero from the history books. The Cuba Che Guevara fought for, is the Cuba Danny wants to escape.

But maybe his is just a story of all young people who want to leave home – to see the world, to check out the Big Elsewhere, entranced by the unknown.

Not the unknown in fact, the slightly and imperfectly known. After all Danny has studied it, not closely, but ardently exchanging his country's sexy swagger and bright clothes for cool black, and logos in English, affecting a most unCuban obsession with health and fitness. Every afternoon when the rest of Cuba dozes, drenched in tropical sleep, Danny runs. He doesn't eat lunch or carbohydrates and is always thinking of ways to make money.

> Che was the sickly asthmatic from the Argentinian upper class
>
> Che was the man whose face is a T-shirt
>
> Che beloved by millions as legend, symbol, saviour
>
> Che's hands – healing hands, fighting hands
>
> Che was the man whose face is a poster
>
> *Shoot, coward, you are only killing a man*

> Che said, *a true revolutionary is guided by love*

> Che struck fear into imperialism's heart

The pink and turquoise buildings which so delight foreigners from grey glass cities, look crass and hick to him. Danny has never lived in cities where advertising billboards sprout like mutant mushrooms, ever bigger and brassier with their pouting painted faces, and sprawling perfect bodies looming down, invading your days and dreams with all the things you don't have and didn't know you needed.

His country's billboards are all faded political slogans. Poignant – the triumphant raised fist: *You can't kill ideas!* Or can you? When you have marketing, advertising, social media… And Danny as the living refutation of *The Revolution will live forever*. Only when we ask him to translate them into English does he appear to even notice them.

> Che made us think it was possible to change the world

> In Bolivia, the enemy outnumbered the guerrillas 3,000 to one

> Che was the man whose face is a beach towel

> When they were hunting for him, the CIA removed all asthma medication from Cuba, from the hospitals, pharmacies and clinics

> Known for his integrity as well as his ideals – Che refused to accept special privileges

> Che would not limit himself to an accident of birth, he fought for the world. But in the Congo and Bolivia he failed
>
> Che, the man whose face is a billboard
>
> *Tu ejemplo Vive. Tus ideas perduran!*
> Your example lives. Your ideas endure!

Maybe a marketing whizz from Uruguay would help them to design advertising to keep the people committed to socialist ideals without just telling them to.

My travelling companion, a compulsive consumer, in a country which proclaims *Production not consumption* as a goal, meets with Danny's approval. She wants to buy everything – from the sexy lace stockings worn by all women in uniform (such a lovely thing on soldiers…), to shoes from the meagre shelves of the government stores, to bags and bags full of bright wooden jewellery from the craft markets.

He watches fascinated to see a shopaholic – someone who gets pleasure from the act of consumption rather than from the goods she is accumulating… Like 'hoarding' and obesity – it is another of capitalism's more bizarre offshoots.

Danny takes us to meet his family, a great compliment and a much more *authentic Cuban experience* than being with the families with the *Casas Particulares* where we stayed, These people have to be rich enough to have a spare room to rent and often have values quite different from the ones the government is espousing – much more materialistic, even quite grasping: *Your skin is so young… Can you send me some face cream? Several jars. Maybe I could sell some…*

> Che is the man whose face was adored
>
> Che was handsome, a romantic, died young
>
> You can't kill transcendence
>
> Che is the man whose face was Smirnoff vodka
>
> Che's hands – when raised in triumph, they shook the world

Danny's is the first house we enter which isn't brightly painted. It is shabby grey concrete, with a miniscule galley kitchen, just a sink and an ancient stove. I can't see a fridge. The backyard was not bedecked with pot plants and greenery like all the vibrant Casas.

Danny is saving to make his mother's house into a Casa with a bathroom and spare room and the ubiquitous rooftop garden for the tourists. When she is established financially, he plans to escape – make his fortune in the tourist industry so he can become a tourist too, visit other countries, go to proper gyms, drink soy decaf lattes in hipster cafés.

If he makes a large fortune he can probably buy organic produce too, not realising that only the rich can afford it in the west. Not realising that they covet the *locally sourced and seasonal* food which is Cuba's staple, and not only very cheap but completely organic – Fidel declared poisoning the soil illegal years ago.

Towards the end of the trip Danny asks if he can 'buy' my iPad. He knows I am a socialist and believe in *From each according to their ability to each according to their need*... I think he presumes I'll give it to him.

I do think about it. I know I am very wealthy compared to him even though I am not at all back home, and cannot afford to simply buy another iPad.

As it is, I tell Danny I can sell it to him, but as he is a capitalist I will apply his principles: the law of supply and demand dictating that I should charge him much more than I paid for it, rather than less…

> Che, who fought against a society that commodifies everything – then became the commodity that helped 'sell' Cuba
>
> Che is now everywhere – on posters and billboards, on T-shirts and beach towels
>
> Che died young – martyred by the CIA, further martyred because they cut off his hands as trophies
>
> Che cannot be killed. He is an idea
>
> Che's hands, healing hands, fighting hands, martyred hands –
> point the way, still

Honk if you love Australia

(banner draped outside suburban house, Australia Day 2011)

One need not love it –
the hot dry shrill,
the white-blue sky.
But the heat-suck
seeps into your soul
despite the wilting.

It may not be love –
but there's always something –
magpies, sprinklers, cicadas
the sharp smell of dry gum leaves
or shorts and long socks
at friendly airports.

One need not love it
and sometimes you don't,
you burn with shame
at Oi Oi Oi
and flag-flavoured warpaint
on stone white skins.

One may not love it
but these kids say they do,
and go to the trouble of telling the world –
Is it Henry Lawson and stoic bushmen;
our clever batsmen? The sunburnt country
and suntanned summers?

Is it vast beaches
not spoiled yet
belonging to no one;
star-bright deserts
and so much wilderness?

Or just peace, light and sky.
Or is it the politics?
Not those pollies
but how we won the eight-hour day;
had the first Labor PM;
and votes for women
way before the 'old country?

No sirs or madams here
we laugh at toffs and blue bloods.
Even our birds
cockatoos, kookaburras –
are lairs and larrikins
They make *me* 'love Australia'.

These kids love it – with their flag
and their handmade sign –
Honk if you love Australia
Innocence, or flag as fence?
Like a US bumper sticker
Your country – leave it or love it

Is this message of love not to us
with our pink skin, blue eyes,
our parents, arriving on earlier boats –
the *original* invaders
but to those recent voyagers –
who have no reason, yet, to love Australia?

But am I being churlish
and they're just Ozzie kids
growing up with beach-house summers –
Dad's a plumber who drives a Merc…
Why wouldn't they love their country?
Why shouldn't they celebrate their luck?

Ask the blackfellas

Lament for a bat

(for Australia after the Cronulla riots 2006)

> *You've copped a bad press small bat*
> *as night creatures often do.*
> *With that first wee hours flutter*
> *I wondered what you were –a butterfly, a tiny bird,*
> une petite chauve souris?
> *Then I loved you – your cartoon ears, old woman face,*

Like all those that love the dark
and shun the gleaming day, they fear you,
Assume you must be kin
to vampires, crows
black cats, witches
Black – and bad

The noxious dark –
pure light's antithesis;
a sordid stain
on white's bright glow;
a shadow over angels' curls –
Good as gold.

Those Pure White Knights of old and new
who fought and fight the darkling scourge
as Hitler did – and they all knew
that dark is evil, black is worse –
black as Moor's skin
dark as Turks' curse.

And we brightly whites?
gleaming clean and sparkling good?
Or are we to you, mere day-time wraiths?
Sickly pale with bloodless shock –
wasted skin denied the light,
Ghost grey, death-white.

> *You weren't so bad, small bat,*
> *bald mouse* – ma petite chauve souris,
> *despite the hype*
> *and the hours you kept.*
> *hanging from the rafters*
> *like a folded fairy umbrella.*
>
> *So when I found your tiny frame*
> *stiff in the curtain's pleats,*
> *I thought of how you hate the light,*
> *and all of them, the dark.*
> *Then I cried – for you, the night,*
> *and the tarnished frightened day.*

Innocent, Ordinary (13 November 2015)

Bags on conveyors, we take off our shoes,
give them our scissors, our nail files, our knives…
Arms in the air in silent surrender
worst part of travelling – this security shit.
Today, there's no grumbling, no indignant complaints
the friendly pat down gives no offence.
We're sombre and nervous, quietly resigned,
just innocent people doing ordinary things.

A black shadow sweeps over the city of light.
This time the innocent victims are 'ours'
in ways all those elsewhere,
are not, though there – it's daily, and thousands,
and of course just as tragic –
innocent people doing ordinary things
killed in the name of a god…

City of poets, city of love,
all of our lives, we've lived there in dreams.
Now it's our own, doing ordinary things,
killed in the name of a god –
a god with no image, brooking no other.
Deluded young martyrs, caliphate schemes
imagined demons – 'prostitutes, pagans',
innocent revellers, Kalashnikov tunes.

We learned French at school,
saw ourselves there – in those white/grey buildings
tall wooden shutters, black lace balconies.
Will those shutters now always be shut?
Will they forgo music events, drink coffee at home
avoid public places, the metro, the movies?
Will their lives forever be shrouded,
dark shadows soaking into their dreams?

Even here, in an airport, so far away –
Please come home it's much safer
I look at these travellers
their ubiquitous wheelies, their jeans and their thongs;
distracting themselves with iPhones, and iPads;
a few bolshie readers with plane-flight-sized books;
toddlers in pushers, clutching their bears,
Innocent people doing innocent things…

Thinking of Home

We'd heard of that country, heard of its hugeness
heard of the miles of empty

A sky full of light so bright it hurts
the earth red and flat and forever

The black dome of night seething with stars
its arking black arms saying welcome

The whole wide country, with so few people
Plenty of room for lost souls

They say they're good people, everyone's equal
Definitely no airs and graces

They laugh at their leaders, no military coups there!
They believe in fair go mate

Looking out for the underdog – that's us!
They say She'll be right, so we will!

Worth all those bullying blue months in the sea's wild claws.
Worth leaving our loved ones, and home…

> But they think we're the people we run from
> We'd disturb their comfortable lives
> They famously fear the dark

Papa he is old, could not be persuaded
I want the devil I know, and that space is all desert,

their hearts, their heads just as empty, And those thousands of stars
are the wrong ones, mocking the distance, the difference

They kick the underdogs, chase them off
send them starving to Somewhere Else

I'd rather face bombs and prison here, than their detention
in the desert or on impoverished islands

They don't want us there. There are car stickers which tell us
'Fuck off we're full'

> They think we're the people we run from
> We'd disturb their comfortable lives
> They famously fear the dark

*

Papa he is scared, he's scared of change
but any change must be better, than the screaming

of bombs, of children and men, skeletal buildings and
the constant fear of the midnight knock…

He sees only the worst, his fears defy reason – A huge rich land.
The Fair Go land. Would they turn us away, fleeing death?

> But they think we're the people we run from
> We'd disturb their comfortable lives
> They famously fear the dark

The Emancipation of the Empty Nest

No daily gaping beak –
all this room – to stretch my wings.

I know who I'm feeding, and the chef's always thanked.
Curries all week, with eggplants and chilli.

No surprise heaters green-glowing all night.
No surprise monster bills to match.

TV locked on ABC. I play *The Messiah* as loud as I like.
Relishing a bit of silence too.

All except one of the towels in the cupboard, not wet on the floor.
How could two people use ten towels?

No more dawn dashes to bus stop in pjs,
or late trips to the station, missing the end of *Midsomer Murders*

No lying awake at two in the morning – 'Are you slumped in an alley,
smashed on the road?' (*You forgot to turn your phone on Mum.*)

*

Now I can wonder in the daytime too –
I wish I'd never heard of Britt Lapthorne.*

I hear you arrived in a snowstorm, the buses on strike,
your carefully planned route ruined.

Alone in the snow in your cool cotton coat, (*It's lined though Mum.*)
I so wish I'd hear you ask *Can you pick me up please?*

I see you poking more coins in the heater:
Use this one – leave it on all night.

As I try to master cooking for one
I think of you with your stale baguette

doing your best to eke out the cheese –
and where will you get your vitamin C?

The silent house cries for *Missy and Pink*
and I ache with the loss of my wandering girl.

I stretch my wings, and they hit the walls.
But I know you'll soar.

*Britt Lapthorne – young Australian backpacker missing presumed murdered in Yugoslavia

Twenty-one monochords for Bry

I was so excited when I thought you had his black curls –
but they told me babies are always dark.

I used to sit and watch you sleep. I understand paintings
called *The Adoration* now.

You were such a joyous child, as if you were packing it all in
early. As if you knew…

While we sat up in bed you'd make up stories called 'Tells'.
You'd give us a list of titles, then pull the chosen one from
under the pillow. And then tell its story.

One of your teachers called you Pixie, and showed your stories
to the Headmaster. We all said you'd be a writer one day.

Your imaginary friends were Shane and his mother Memory.
Do imaginary friends usually have Mothers?

You and your dad played a game where you were Barney and
Taxi. I can't remember who was which or why.

You were angry with me for not telling you – *if I'd have
known I could have stopped him. He would have stopped for me.*

Your wonderful drawings – their design, their humour, their
magic. I said you'd be an artist one day.

You memorised a whole Zulya song in Tartar Russian – I cry
when I hear it now.

I can't go out, I look too ugly. But we're in Paris. *Especially in Paris.*

In Prague, when I thought we'd run out of money,
you tried to cheer me up by singing.

First day at high school, the sight of those small stoic shoulders.

You were Romeo's Juliet with 'Rodney from Warrandyte
Glass'. They all said you should be on the stage.

I'd never heard of 'school refusal'. I soon found out.

Belly button, nose, eyebrow, neck, lips – what's the statement
– tough, ugly, untouchable? But you were still so beautiful.

You discovered a whole new chapter on the way to the exam.

Mum, I'm not into boys.

When I came out of hospital you bought me the 'softest
towel in the shop'.

You said you were homesick even before you left.

Twenty-one can't be such a milestone – if it was, I would be
with my Briony T who's over the sea.

A Short History of Hair (apologies to Li Po)

When I was small
I had hair to my waist
I flitted with fairies and smiled at the world
You always sang
Like the sigh of a breeze

When I grew more
And Dad was my mate
My hair was cut off, and I was a boy
You never told me
That boys had more fun

When I was seven
I drowned in the world
I drowned in the world – a world without Dad
You never told me
The demons would win

When I was fourteen
I hid in my room
I hid in my room and I hated my life
You never knew
I was so alone

Now that I'm older
My hair's long again
I've had his name tattooed on my skin
So I won't forget him. You don't always win

Faith, love, justice and so forth…

(Quote from manager of a Catholic club when asked what Catholic clubs stand for)

1. *Catholics Catholics, ya, ya, ya*

Orda-be, orda-be dipped in tar. Exotic as Bedouins In long flowing robes,
Smoke swinging, spell chanting. *They know the words*
In squeaky WASP Canberra there are 'Catholics' and 'Publics'
(*Orda-be, orda-be dipped in gold*.) My mother says
they do all that breeding, to take over the world

Rory O'Leary

Rory O'Leary is a good bloke, church every Sunday with his eight kids
Does not hit his Kathleen, or not very often, drinks only on Friday and then not that much.
But he does like a flutter (he knows about heaven) would bet on two flies crawling on shit.
He likes the gee-gee's, bets every Saturday.
Mostly comes home with a very long face. Occasionally, flowers.

2. You are a sinner. Confess! Now you're not.

It is the Good Time Church, 'party every night church'. They know how to have fun.
Drinking and Gambling and Swearing and Fighting.
Wild roaring men, of course they are flawed.
But then they confess, and it all goes away
Bless me father for I have sinned...

Rory O'Leary

Then his club gets the pokies. Just a bit of fun really.
They make so much money.
And we give it all back. It is special, his club, just for the chosen.
This is his treat, his piece of heaven. You have to be Catholic, you know the words.
It's a free country. We don't make them do it. Bless me father for I have sinned

3. Praise the Lord and Pass the Ammunition

It will all be all right with God on our side. Our machines are named
Suffer Little Children, Our Lady of Sorrows. The punchier ones are
Avarice and Greed. They cross themselves when they pull the lever.
Bless me father for I have sinned – I've just blown the rent money what do I do?
But whose side is God on – the clubs' side or *theirs*?

Rory O'Leary

He loves the excitement, the lights and the jingles. His special
machine named Gun Totin' Cowboy. Stetsons and spurs and Billy the Kid –
Gives it a stroke each night for luck. And sometimes it works. Old Billy comes good.
But more often than not he is endlessly pouring… *My turn soon* churning round in his brain.
And when he gets home, he's lying again

4. On Earth as it is in Heaven

It's the Jackpot church. *One day I'll win*. No harm in a dream
We are the chosen, we know the words. You might have a shit life –
too many kids, not enough time or love or money. But at the end of the tunnel
there's a chink of blue sky where someone else cooks and nobody cries.
No grog and no bets, just flowers and song – I can put up with *this*, for a future of *that*.

Rory O'Leary

Oh it's just what men do. He's bit of a show-off, always taking a risk.
Just a bit of fun really, no harm in a dream. Rory's a good man, I often get flowers.
I don't like the club, it leads them astray. They think it's OK, with God on their side.
You'd think that our priests could see what they do when they see that mad gleam,
as they pour it all in. *One day, you know, we might even win.*

5. Faith, love, justice and so forth…

No, there's no problems here – we'd know if there was.
We know all our punters, they're part of the flock. Yes, of course we do care,
it's part of our creed. *We know the words*. But nor will we stop them
Free Country you know – we want no nanny state.
What do you mean it might be too late?

Rory O'Leary

Rory O'Leary was a good bloke. He loved his Kathleen and all of his kids
But his club got the pokies, *and he knew the words*.
He tried to control it, staying away. But they had him captured, got into his
blood, sucked out his soul and all that was good *He went to confession
he knew the words. Bless me father for I have sinned*. But nobody heard.

Bad luck

They say *with cancer it's about 80% bad luck.*

Forget the burnt bacon and coffee,
the mouldy cheese, the microwave –
it is largely luck.
With stress/junk food/chemical additives
thrown in.

So it is with life. You don't have to believe in fate
to know a random branch can hit your car
a bushfire can choose your house or miss it,
'external economic forces' can make you rich or send you broke.
You can be born with an addictive personality or not.

You can marry the wrong person, mix with the wrong crowd,
accept the wrong advice, take the wrong road.
Some learn 'the hard way' but survive, wiser.
Some learn without the 'hard way', some don't
Good sense? Good advice? Gook luck?

*

They say *they have to hit rock bottom*

She remembers his sexy eyes
his wild bolshiness
his commitment to 'the struggle'
Twenty years later, demons met and not,
She sees him, remembers…

Two young men – charming Irish rogues
Attracted to both, one is persistent, and she marries him.
It is love and homes and babies
happily briefly after.
Wrong time, wrong choice, addictive personality.

Two young men – rock bottom/homeless
One lands, scrapes up, claws back.
The other, the husband, keeps falling…
Job, love, family, health all tumbling too
Wrong advice, wrong turns, addictive personality

*

They say *it's in the genes*

Her wrong choice to love wild Irish boys
with addictive personalities like her dad,
who says to her when he is sick of life,
that the only thing worth living for
is whiskey.

And when he plans to die
Though she doesn't know it yet
Sends her out to buy whiskey
He says, with an emphasis she misses
You'll need two bottles

Now she regularly writes lists:
'Things worth living for':
Poetry, music, friends, daughters,
commitment to 'the struggle',
Mostly it works.

*

They say *who knows when we could turn*?

But just say it didn't, and whiskey won?
It could, she knows it could.
It has always been with her, in her black pit:
her solace, her oblivion. Her rock bottom?
Wrong time, wrong genes.

Bad luck?

Things of Wood and Iron

Wood

The small jarrah table with gnarled legs
topped with a slice of polished trunk
shaped like a rough artist's palette
sits by the pot-belly, perfect for a book
and a glass, at the end of the day
or by the fire in the winter
He rarely slowed down enough to use it

The squat ironbark candlestick,
rough then smooth
the tapered neck emerging gracefully
from cliffed sides.
Not very functional, the hole too small
for most candles, and the wax-drip spoiled the wood

The mirror frame
in spiky walnut
ridged with whorls and swirls, like the nut
He looked at it, never in it
Never vain, not interested in surfaces

The stringy-bark bush chair
imperious by the front door
bought for him to celebrate their arrival
we're in the bush, you need a bush chair!
He never sat in it, couldn't see himself
as Lord of the Manor

The grand Dattner table –
(Tasmanian Messmate) they bought together
They'd borrowed so much for the house
what's another two thousand? he said.
It's just pretend money
So it was

Iron

He had a thing about shoe-lasts,
one of those quirks that made her love him.
So she looked out for them in junk shops
to add to the collection.
Now they huddle around his tree
like a clutch of bewitched trolls

The metal Gandalf goblet
bought because she saw a resemblance:
long thin face, wise eyes, sometimes secretive
stem of twisted beard, hard to grasp.
He was a beer drinker, never used it
and it made her wine taste sour

His favourite here, was not her gift
but a quirky gift from me,
nod to his wild Irishness:
an IRA horse-spike –
a twist of nails – reminding him of the real…

His final gift for her – a set of candles, black.
She used to light one on the anniversary
The last one sits unlit beside his photo
in its small driftwood frame

The River Keepers

(The Yarra patchwork quilt, Warrandyte)

We are the river keepers.
Not serious men in waders
who measure E. coli counts
and record platypus sightings.

We women keep river memories,
sewing the flow, droplets of dreams:
solemn spirals – Wurrundjeri stories
stitched on felt in ochres, tans.

Glimpses through windows:
wattles trail fingers,
scatter gold on brown satin;
water dimples like beaten metal;

lone white duck shines through
folds of greens, greys;
mist-looming ghost trunks
fringe sleepy water.

(The mist was difficult – hard to pin down:
strips of net, layer upon layer;
or puffs of wool trying to hover;
or transparent fabric – brown murmur beneath)

We stitch the seasons' stories:
Summer, where stones rise while water sinks;
Winter, soft swathes floating over river-glass;
Spring, and she's urgent, swollen, rushing with joy.

We have no *people* in our quilt
No duck-stuffers, dog-shitters
or well dressed joggers
ears plugged – deaf to river-song,

We sew a pristine river, a benign river.
No despairing dead flowers –
clutched to tree breasts.
The river will keep this friend.

None of that.
Just crisp wisp-filled mornings,
calm floating evenings.
Water like stitching –

cleansing, calming,
continuing.

Mother who gave me life

(1) Earth

I remember warm dark days
before-days, when comfort-coiled
I wait for signs – drips of damp
tempting my tightness. Slowly I unfold,
stretch. Now I know there is an Up
to aim for – I straighten, thrust.
Suddenly this burst of bright.
Mother releases me.

I don't remember this being part of the deal.
Just going about my business with sun
and rain, my green slow-grow.
So what's this on the wind – the devil's mad brew?
We grow too fast, too tall, all show,
roots too weak,
all goodness gone.
Mother won't be pleased.

And here we have her vengeance
Think you can bend me to your will?
Damn you and your poisonous greed.
Groans, roars and cracks
wide open, gaping wound to be plugged
by them and all their detritus.
But who will survive her wrath? Why me.
She is my mother – I am reborn.

Terrible and blessed are the powers of Earth.

(2) Fire

Can we imagine a place
where it is purely benign?
A light in the darkness,
a welcoming glow –
slow spread of warmth, thawing the bones.

Could they understand
it is always a threat –
constantly licking the fringes of life,
pervasive presence,
slow fizzing fuse…

Can we remember
it's working for us?
Deep underground it is roaring away.
Subterranean scaffold
of our comfortable life.

Could *they* believe
as they toast by their fires, that
some of us are afraid of our trees…
Are you our friends – or
compliant torches awaiting the flame?

Can we conceive
of trusting again?
Enjoying the heat, lapping up sun –
when summer's just summer,
not bushfire season?

They will see
their harmless hearth dragon
a whimsy, a plaything.
comforting, harmless
its puff of warm breath.

In *our* bush every summer
that creature can grow…
far beyond Disney nightmares –
the fiend belching flame,
looming down from the sky.

Can we imagine
ever trusting again?

Terrible and blessed are the powers of fire.

(3) Water

Oldest of elements:
She is sweat, snow, rivers, tears
Earth blood, life blood

We're all from her sea, and sea of the womb
She is dew, hail, dribble, piss
She murmurs, drips, trickles. She roars.

Tied to the moon – to the making of life
She's thrashing oceans and tranquil lakes
The mist-kissed morn and the rain-slashed night

The treasured drop that promises more
She's the pounding gift to the thankful field
Her power harnessed in dams and wheels

Tsunami, monsoon, hurricane, flood
She cleanses, drenches, quenches, drowns
Earth blood, life blood

Nothing can halt the force of her power
She can carve canyons, mould mountains
Turn sleepy creeks into wild inland seas

She can also withdraw
So we're craving each drop
Do you think you can squander, poison, and plunder – forever?

Terrible and blessed are the powers of water

(4) Air

A gasp and a squawk as you take her in,
the very first act of your brand new life,
drawing her into your tiny lungs.
Coal to heart's furnace.

And you go on from there – oblivious.
She's omnipresent, invisible
taken for granted – except
when your lungs have to fight.

Sometimes you'll notice
she's sick, so sick –
when what you're breathing's
so bad you taste it.

And when you escape,
you notice what's missing,
and you relish the absence…
no smell, or taste.

Though you *can* feel her,
with her summer hints, alive and soft,
pollen-pulse and seed-shift.
Tantalising kiss, wafting glimpse…

She can turn lusty, full of life
breathing hot and hard
she'll suck you dry,
turn cool, send respite, or not –

She can be Lilith
all thrashing rage.
Without reason, warning, she will
lash, rip, destroy all she's sustained.

She swirls around us
as life goes on –
our flighty friend.

Terrible and blessed are the powers of air.

Conversations with Katharine

Spiders?

Little sisters – part of my life
They dispatch the mossies, they're saving the books
Watched this one for ages, spinning her magic,
But can you take her outside? Karen gets worried.

Television?

Why would I want one, there is so much else.
Nasty invader, an alien voice.
I choose my companions, to nourish and teach.
So many books and so little time.

Gifts?

I'm sorry I gave the teapot away. He admired it so much,
he has very little, and it made him so happy.
(*The red Finnish teapot, I bought it for her
saved all my money, but she didn't know that.*)

Décor?

I know that it worries them, this hole in my wall.
it came from the earthquake. Just our small shudder.
I like to see it, the light coming in.
It gives me some comfort to know I'm still here.

Music:

How insulting to Beethoven, just being noise,
You must do him justice, sit quiet and listen.
In the still of the evening there is nothing better
'The Moonlight', a sherry, the 'Fremantle Doctor'.

Life:

Fight for what's right, be true to yourself.
Don't be beguiled by tinsel and surface.
Make some small difference
Sow in the soul of man, one thought that won't die.

The Majesty of Trees

You laugh at our howl at the moon – you might call it lunacy
to raise up our voices to praise the sublime

which is now, all of this   this earthly sublime…
We don't suffer a bad life for the promise of paradise.

When we die, there's no Peter await at the gate.
We're one with the worms, complete the circle.
Though we too, have our chants:
May you never hunger, may you never thirst.

There's no 'God Almighty' though some can't let go,
and make her female. Definitely no churches. No phallic spires

We have the Majesty of Trees. Of old,
we are humbled by them. Here, we might even kneel.

But you chopped them all down, left us a branch
for your angels and stars, to celebrate your 'virgin birth' story.

We too love our holy days, our solstices, sabats
where we honour the elements, celebrate seasons

not woman-become-vessel birthing man-become-god, who dies
and is reborn, and in whose name six million were burned.

And now, the Disney dirt-job:
cackling hags astride straw brooms

so countless children now fear old women,
who may occasionally, for excellent reasons –

howl at the moon…

Official Memories, Official Lies

(for Hugo Vivian Throssell – VC)

Jim never marched on Anzac Day
He didn't need an 'official day'

Whitewashing his memories
It was there in his head, the blood

And the mud. He wanted it over
They gave him a medal:

> *Exceptional Bravery* – the highest war honour
> They thought they had bought him
> That he'd sing their song, their wind-up war hero
> Whom they could trot out:
> *War is good for national pride*

But he stunned all those Tories – the jingoist gentry,
his family amongst them – *The war has made me a socialist*

*

Hugo Vivian (Jim for short)
Strong, good looking, great footy hero

Stoic, laconic, great sense of humour
Full of that spirit we now called 'Anzac'

He was also no fool, saw what they were doing
Comfy old men sending young men to die

Steep jagged cliffs – the Turks at the top
Trenches so close, they could throw the bombs back

Generals ordering suicide missions
Line after line of young men mown down

Farmers and postmen, dentists and clerks
Some were just school boys…

Who wouldn't return with a hatred of war?

> But they gave him a medal
> The highest war honour
> They thought they had bought him
> That he'd sing their song
> They could trot him out
> Their wind-up war hero
> *War is good for national pride*

The good men of Northam couldn't believe it
No son of our soil would betray us like that

They all turned their backs – his family, his country
He couldn't get work, constantly shunned

Making it hard   to fight the depression
Making it hard   just to survive

Had they forgotten
They gave him a medal?

Exceptional Bravery – For Valour, it said
Multiple wounds, refusal to leave

His men who he argued all deserved medals
He didn't think he did anything special

And now, nor did they. They wanted him gone,
They meant him forgotten

*

Jim's family don't march for him in April
The day we honour (some of) our soldiers

We don't need memorials to help us remember
We remember *all* of his bravery –

The blood of Hill 60
The fight for his country,

The courage to stand up to a crowd
To speak against war surrounded by 'warriors'

We remember his country's rejection
The people who shunned him

They meant him forgotten,
They wanted him gone –

And he went

Duar River Poems

Another Eden

Duar River – January

She slithers through our city dreams
Black and cold as midnight whips,
Taunting flash of sluttish red –
Dark alleys, coiled shadows

In the bush, we're on her patch
She's curled, waiting
Neck-prickling presence in the grass
Slight rustle, quick flick

She joins us in the silken creek
Soft 'S' in gleam of brown
Sticks and bark quiver, pretend –
Chase us out, barely wet

Casuarinas, feather light
Bellbirds plink down stony slopes
Blurry stillness – nearly dusk.
A little patch of Eden

Leadlight windows in the house:
Greens and greys of shifting leaves.
In the curve of the snaking creek
A sneaky flash of black and red

We have to block the gappy doors
With 'wind sausages'
To keep her out (and all the rest)
She'd only come in for the cool

Sylvie says, adding that her door
Is never locked. *She's* not deterred,
Or other friends: lizards, bats, spiders
And the odd lost chook

There is no key, no need.
Just city dreams –
Nightmares from another Eden,
We need to keep at bay.

If she really has to…

The tiny blue-rimmed cottage,
front wall opening as a door
reminds me of a childhood
picture of the house where Peter Pan
and Wendy lived with the Lost Boys.
Wall opens to candlelit room
warm, glowing…
Dark woods glower in the distance.

She's made it her own:
her felt and silk paintings hang
bravely on the stamp-sized walls
of this house/room for one.
And he's there in her home
on the hill, by the river
with its five rooms, running water
and her son.

But you left. No woman leaves her child
he says smug in her kitchen,
cooking on the stove
that I bought for her.
You chose to leave, he says, playing her
music, reading her books.
Women only leave,
if they really have to.

So she and I have our meals
from the esky, in the garden –
it's a bit of a crowd inside, with two.
Cutely cosy, if you don't mind
the squash and not washing.
But he's up there on the hill…
The river murmurs its disquiet –
A woman only leaves if she really has to.

Everything is ominous

Long wet grass by the water
full of surprises between your toes – then the blood.

Silky brown river
where red-bellied black snakes also swim.

Like *Picnic at Hanging Rock* –
too much serenity has an edge.

The occasional gravel-rumble of a distant car.

She reminds me to always check
my shoes before I slip my feet into them.

The idea that absence
can be so tangible – and portentous.

In the otherwise quiet
the click-rattle of trees slowly shedding, dropping.

An approaching car in the empty night.

Strange lumps on your body housing
small bloodsuckers. At least ticks leave no mess.

That temperamental river –
One large downpour and we're stranded.

The strange act
of straining for sound.

Listening through bird clamour for car rumble, gate creak

The enormous lace monitor*
who's 'just after the chickens'.

The scrabbling rats in the roof
near the bed – I wouldn't mind possums…

The puncture of night at the sound of a car and
conversation that stops till it disappears

Still the silence is ominous

---

* lace monitor – indigenous goanna – grows to six feet long, can eat chickens, cats, and small dogs

The Dialectics of Rain

Rain is pounding, river's swelling, banks are sliding, branches drooping. Damp keeps seeping…

rain-forest: a forest full of rain –
each entangled tree blending into the next

dark primaeval spikes of Zamia ferns
straight white streaks of candlebarks

bark strips tossed casually over their arms –
the most elegant of long grey scarves

the joyous dawn chorus – tweets and twitters
whoops, shrieks and soaring scales:

whipbirds and wonga pigeons, blue wren
and his scuttling brown harem –

so comfortable in their acknowledged space
they're almost tame

midsummer, and we love a wet bushfire season
grateful for the surprise of lush and green

and that friendly brown river wraps us in
cool arms, floats us under feathered casuarinas…

*

but it's still raining, the river turns nasty –
flowing meaner, faster, slowly closer

trapping us with tick-dropping trees, leech-ridden grass and
the regular drip into a red plastic bucket beside the bed

a small brown frog in my water glass this morning
and the edgy company of a dingo howling in the hills

now we dread each dripping hour, unless the days
turn tropical, the damp living in our skin:

four o'clock and a tense sky broods
a rumbling preamble to the thundering downpour

which when suddenly turned off, clears the air
as predictable and cleansing as an evening G and T

but still the sly twine, the seeping damp and I'm sure
that vine wasn't creeping round the handrail yesterday

what was once the dawn's enchanting fanfare
is now a raucous cacophony,

screeching, discordant, as it all closes in
the repeated single note of the wonga pigeon, harping

sinister, like an angry dripping tap when you know
the tank is nearly empty

Into the Wild Woods

The woods are dangerous for grannies
wolves slink into their houses and eat them
then dress in their clothes!
Woods are full of dangerous grannies:
bony fingers beckon children to gingerbread houses
and then they eat them.
Other grannies have houses on hen's feet!
How big were those hens? And where are their heads?

Where is the light in this velvet gloom?
Even the trees loom and glower
scrawny arms reach out, claws scrape…
You sense the creatures out this time of night
aren't friends, though they may be merely wary,
don't like clomping intruders in their special places.
And we know there are no wolves or bears. Not in this story, anyhow.

But there are darker forces in the woods at night
strange beings from an older time
who collude with thickets,
guide you down lost paths
to deadly marshes, with eerie lights
but it's really just a bit of play
and no one's hurt – you find your way.
In this story anyhow.

In fact, think of these woods
on a dappled summers day – twinkling streams
where Ondine lives, and she's like them –
nice in the daytime.
The creatures now seem cute!
Fluffy tails, stripy backs, snuffling and scampering.
And we're not scared of weasels and squirrels.
Not in this story, anyhow.

Do we have woods Mummy
where there are houses with hens feet
and wolves who eat grannies?
No, we have the Bush, and some very shy snakes.
Houses have stumps, hens stand on feet,
Grannies are tough,
and are friends with the snakes.
In this story, anyhow.

Villanelle on an MRI

You know they're only making sure
Eliminating from the list
A precaution – nothing more

But that smothering tomb, deafening roar…
Nuclear medicine, worth the risk?
You know they're only making sure

Sliding down its shining maw
clamping down, a metal fist
Just a precaution, nothing more

Test tube body, count the score
of wayward cells and tumours, cysts…
You know they're only making sure

He could be back, he's been before
What if this bad moon persists?
A precaution, nothing more

Potential outcomes – can't ignore
Memory stirs, invaders lurk
You know they're only making sure
Just a precaution, nothing more

France Poems

The Dance (for Katie)

*Two days' flight and two years' pay
it'll take to see her now.*

Even though you always knew
the process of her being
was also one of going, still
you can't believe she's 'gone'.

From the very start
all our lives a dance –
bonding, separation. A courtly minuet –
together, apart, together.

At first we dance to nursery rhymes
twirling in as one.
Then abyss of adolescence,
wall-flowers – parents shunned.

Daughter becomes stranger –
swirling out of sight.
Not fair! I hate you.
Apart, apart, apart.

And now, there's this vast distance,
these very foreign shores –
this is going much too far
Going, going, gone.

*Two days' flight and two years' pay
it'll take to see her now*

And how will you be my dear one?
Forever *Australian in Paris – alone and lonely?*
Always the other, *Almost French*,
only almost happy?

Or will you swathe yourself in a Paris cloak?
Just like you used to sleep, like a small brown bear
blanket-burrowing so completely
none of you showed.

My little Virgo, so fastidious, thorough
always a thinker, an 'examined life'…
Paris becomes you, its intellect, style.
You never liked our laid-back life.

So will you see us
as the philistine outpost –
cricket, football, reality TV
Barbed wire fences in harsh red deserts?

You have *cuisine, culture, civilisation*,
a country which honours philosophers, poets.
And my darling girl,
though the dance slows with distance

it won't ever stop.
You'll hold out your hand – *This dance?*
and I'll save for two years,
fly for two days –

Together, apart
together.

Petit Poulet a la Russe – a family culinary history

Mama hated cooking –
was never taught, her mother didn't care.
Mama was an artist, lived in Paris once,
ate her meals in smoky cafes,
with *beaucoup du vin rouge*

In another life we ate her wifely fare:
chops, carrots, peas; sausages and mash;
Friday fish, and frozen chips.
But Father cooked on Saturdays: Pasta! Rice!
Curry with coconut, and bananas.

Fussy younger siblings soon began to whinge:
They said the food was strange.
Dad sulked, took away his whisk and bowl
Mama was annoyed. She didn't get to go on strike,
because customers complained.

Now Dad's mother was a cook
She'd been to Russia, brought back
Petit Poulet a la Russe: chicken, bacon
almonds, asparagus. No cabbage, dumplings?
More Français than Russe…

She showed how much she loved us
with little gifts of food –
on our breakfast plates when we came to stay:
jams from her garden – fig for Dad, apricot for me
and for Mum, her golden cape gooseberry.

Her special porridge:
dates, apples, honey, wheat germ.
(Remember wheat germ?)
Health food before her time,
she and Gaylord Hauser.*

Petit Poulet du Mama had
bacon rolls with toothpicks
almonds from a packet, asparagus from a tin,
the whole thing swamped in white sauce,
A glug of sherry – her *je ne sais quoi*

Foods of the World arrived – the first one *France*
Time-Life changed our lives. Dad sneered. *Yanks?*
Teaching us to cook! But I was hooked:
picnics with pâté, baguettes, brie
meals of soufflés, crêpes, quiche…

Mama was delighted, though perplexed.
Could not understand the fuss.
My *Petit Poulet*: fresh asparagus, prosciutto,
chicken breasts – marinated, char-grilled
A vodka toast: *Salut La Russe*!

The dish moves on once more, to France.
My daughter cooks it her way when I stay –
asparagus and almonds from her garden…
She enfolds it all in pastry, adds camembert and cream,

She's a vego now, it's become *sans poulet*!

petit poulet a la Russe – little chicken in the Russian style
beaucoup du vin rouge – lots of red wine
du Mama –-Mama's version
je ne sais quoi – a mysterious special touch
sans poulet – without chicken

* Gaylord Hauser – health food guru, popular in the 1950s, promoted yoghurt, molasses, and wheat germ…

'*Le Temps Perdu*' (apologies to Proust)

> Real time is a figment of the imagination. Imaginary time is real. (Stephen Hawking)

Of course we're always mucking round with time –
A friend used to say whenever
daylight saving started,
it was a free day for the bosses.

So what if you died
before you got your day back?
What if I died before I returned home?
One day of my life lost…

Time Lost (Flight QR 905 Melbourne – Paris)

So again I lose a day –
I'm listening to a Wednesday
radio programme on the ABC 'live'
and it's Thursday.

I know where it went –
slipped behind the orange rim
of a continuous sunset –
the day the sunset ate.

I keep sliding the blind to check
and yes – it's still sunset, hours of it.
Hours swallowed, then spread
molten across the horizon.

That's why we have two breakfasts
five hours apart. First the orange juice
lumpy egg and flat croissants,
A 'day' later, hungry for dinner, wine…

No – juice, yoghurt and unspeakable coffee.
Why? It's got to be evening.
Clearly not. Two mornings –
two breakfasts to bookend those lost hours.

Time Frozen

And now, that day's in limbo, waiting,
Flying past that bright slice of sky
Is it another day at home, ticking off lists:
packing, bills, garden, post?

Or is it a Paris day, a could-be day
of cobbles, bistros, avenues of budding chestnut?
Or a Chartres day, recovering with loving daughter
Chez Elle, spring rain on shining tiles?

Time Bent (*Rue des Grandes Filles Dieu Chartres* 2015)

This day should be night.
This spring should be autumn.
I keep my phone on home time
to explain my body's confusion.

Especially as I have a birthday here
which has already happened there.
(Birthday wishes on Facebook.)
So here, I'm still 65 – a day, or a year, younger.

It's always autumn on my birthday –
soft rain on sodden leaves, starting to stack
the wood by the door, another blanket on the bed.
Pumpkins, persimmons, pomegranates…

Not here, where for three weeks I'm a day younger.
It's buttercups and freesias, snow peas and asparagus
Bright shoots defying icy ground,
the first feel of milky sun, on starved white skin.

Time Warped/Shrunk (Napier Street Fitzroy 1981)

Now time plays new tricks:
Mothering starts afresh. Rewind
thirty-five years…recall that selfless skin
the world narrowing, closing in.

Days reduced to small messy moments:
filled with cleaning – bodies, clothes, plates, floors.
Though machines whirr daily there's no machine
for wriggling, squealing *don't-want-to-get-in/out* bodies.

Bath time either a sea of boat
and duck-filled tranquillity: damp neck curls
fluffy towels on silky skin, lavender and lullabies,
or a trip to Mt Doom, complete with Orcs and Nasguls.

I am thirty, she is three. My lounge room is
festooned with nappy flags, floors a sticky toy
minefield. No flowers, pottery, nothing of mine –
the chaotic house, a child shrine.

Time Running Out, Slipping Away Flying (1981)

You long for more than moments, slabs
not slivers…

        to read a whole page

        to finish

a whole

                        sentence

        to sleep

more than

                        two hours

at a time

        to finish

a movie   without
        nodding

                            off

You imagine
the most perfect gift in all the world: a pink-ribboned box
marked

Hours and hours… ALL FOR YOU

Time Gained (Flight QR 982 Paris–Melbourne)

And I didn't die, taking my lost day with me.
Must have been dozing as it slowly slipped back.
After hours of squashed-limbs-eyes-shut-trying
head aching from a year's worth of miniature movies –

When it felt like it should have been morning,
I anticipate breakfast with unspeakable coffee –
No, we're served dinner, and good Aussie wine…
Of course, my day – back again!

And now I'm home, I'm the right age.
It's morning and autumn, and I'm in my own bed
Untold hours and minutes to use
Le Temps Perdu, je l'ai trouvé!

'French country living'

Old men in berets with interesting faces
earnestly explaining in a series of close-ups
the secrets of truffles, the skinning of frogs.
They meander on bicycles down cobbled lanes,
baguette upright like a crusty flag.

Beautiful of course,
though too much spin –
the cuisine, the markets, all that 'Chic.'
This book would enthuse me
about her new home –
Those picture-book photos:

Long thin windows with white wooden shutters
tiny iron balconies, festooned with red flowers
winding streets with glowing patisseries –
(rows and rows of those trusty baguettes)
spring fields full of flowers – primroses, snowdrops
and those bleak winter trees beguiling in mist.

Prodigal daughter home for a visit,
The bush sighs its welcome
our bright sky is blue
And our solace for winter –
the low bowing wattles
spreading gold at her feet.

Teeming street markets
resplendent with produce
in quaint wicker baskets
with handwritten signs
exotic vegies – celeriac, radiccio,
eight sorts of haricots, whole stalls of cheese

I had trained my maggies
to visit for breakfast
chortling their glorious welcome on cue.
When I was away, that call,
joyful yet plaintive, so full of longing
was for me, a call home…

The air full of perfume – boronia, mint
rain-wet eucalyptus.
Paint splash visits from lorikeets, rosellas.
All the bush shining
with grey-green glints.
Look – it's winter, and all this green!

And yet,
each time I saw her –
there she was reading,
head down, oblivious
to our wonderful show.
That infernal old man with his hat and his bread

On the couch, on the table,
in the garden, by the loo –
dog-eared, well-thumbed –
French Country Living.
Totally smitten –
my 'homesick' girl.

The River Won't Keep This Friend

(apologies to Missy Higgins)

(May 1996)

We thought the river was our haven
sometimes unpredictable.
Hidden depths could turn her nasty
You had to be prepared.

But still, we thought this was the place
and we were there, lulled by soothing murmurs,
that balmy autumn when we told you.
River of solace, river of consolation.

We thought it would bring back happy times:
dawn walks through glinting gums, cakes at the Bakery,
picnic teas on sultry nights – drinks cooling in the shallows.
River of sparkling dimples, river of cool relief.

It seemed to have worked, there were no tears.
You were calm, solemn, asked Serious Questions:
Why would he leave me? What will we do?
But you already knew – (that schoolyard hiss)…

Then it seemed chameleon friend turned.
Water flowed darker, faster.
Murmurs have a hint of menace.
Treacherous autumn. The river knows.

Gripped with some strange fear
I felt her pull, saw you drawn
to her dark magnet, and she to yours.
Hungry river, seeking friends. River of bad tidings.

Calling, calling. Ondine beckons.
Sorrow drowning, weightless wafting.
Lure of sleep forever green.
River of sweet escape.

No. You were just lost in your sad world
bowed by a weight not meant for small shoulders
It was I who heard the siren song, briefly glimpsed another path
River of reverie, release…

River of consolation, solace
But no release for now
Not this time a sweet escape –

The river won't keep this friend.

the car, the boxes

(January 2016)

>   not thinking of Pandora
>   you speak of the car, the boxes
>   not thinking of what would crawl out:

death dragged out of safe abstraction
by his own hand no longer merely literary
I see that hand taking the hose, stealing
the pills, drinking the whisky
turning on the ignition. I see him

packing the boxes, his life into boxes
why did he need them? was there a chance
he'd change his mind? his battered old clothes?
his diary in that tiny writing
all those lists of things to do, IOUs?

it was on our block, our retreat, our happy place
our bit of bush, wombats and stringy-barks
he loved the fire, had it lit early morning
brought me my tea while he cooked the eggs
did he choose it on purpose, like choosing the date?
no, all he could possibly plan was escape

having been long banished, the image creeps in:
the car, the boxes, the body
deep in the bush, our bush
I knew where he'd be by the postmark
yes of course they arrived too late
we were warned not to 'view' him

carbon monoxide makes a terrible mess
so my image is more benign:
his head slumped over the wheel
the mop of black curls I loved
in the car with the boxes

Easter Toll

Gold and silver shine and glitter
give them chocolate, give them sugar.

How we love them, watch them quiver
scouring honeyed hiding places.

Lots of rabbits reproducing
laying eggs that last forever.

Pile them up in mounds of plenty,
pile them up on groaning tables.

Moaning Jesus hanging up there,
smiling Jesus full of love.

Creeping cars on crawling freeways, petrol stations
of the cross, fill your faces while you're waiting.

Angry drivers full of chocolate,
angry Romans full of hate.

And we die of too much eating,
kill ourselves with too much rage.

Easter takes too great a toll.
Give us back benign Ostara –

Yet another ritual plundered.
Corrupted then, with cant and greed

And all they did for celebration
was drink some wine, and plant some seed.

PowerPoint (an informative talk to family violence workers)

Power, domination, control
the crux of it all…
Six foot four in his size twelve shoes
he didn't seem so huge as he munched
his muesli bar, setting up his PowerPoint

Presentation which demonstrated how his unit
had improved the stats on family violence
in our community   tells us green girls
it was all about power, *domination and control*
You would be amazed…

He spruiked on *the increase in*
prosecution of perpetrators who are now
feeling the iron fist of the law
lots of proud stats, many achievements,
(god, coppers onside, achievement enough)

Asking for questions which he clearly
didn't want because he guesses we all knew
police stations not so understanding
who weren't committed, didn't care
or were downright hostile…

But our questions weren't:
they were polite, careful, gently inquiring,
asking advice: *how can I get my local
station to…what would you do if…*
One woman told of an incident in which
(as background to the story)
the cops were an hour late…
Our man flipped
became an outraged adolescent
a truculent two-year-old with a monster

tantrum *How dare you!*
I'm not a punching bag for the state police
Not good enough, Insulted, I'm Leaving…
She, polite worker (unpaid)
Ten years experience on the front line

abjectly sorry over and over.
He wouldn't back down
kept on and on about *Being insulted*
Had enough… Standing over her –
six foot four in his size twelve shoes

Then he left, took his bat and ball and left
halfway through his presentation on
the police commitment to the eradication
of family violence
leaving a silent room full of shocked women

many with tears in their eyes for their
colleague who was weeping
who had put herself into dangerous places
so many times, like this one –
an injured woman, her traumatised kids,

cowering together behind the couch
and because the cops were an hour late
he terrorised them all some more
for that very long hour
then got away

How to untie a tie (for Rhonda)

There are two kinds of power – power-over, power-within
(Starhawk *Dreaming the Dark*)

What strange things ties are:

A piece of fabric twisted noose-like around the neck.
Sad skinny thing, flopping, dangling...

Apparent vulnerability – belying reality.
If a wise person were to ask what this tie is for* –

I would have to say, it doesn't do anything.
It is not even decorative. But it stands for a lot:

Sets apart the white collar from the blue singlet,
physical power from the kind which leaves no bruises,

not on the body anyhow... But still Power-over.

*

But we have Power-within – Immanence.
Within is where our wings wake –

a small seed, a flutter. They grow, these little buds –
a flicker, a whisper:

I am good, I am strong. Power-within is its own furnace.
Small curled feathers stretch, grow

*I have always been good,
I can always be strong.*

*

Wings are everything a tie is not – except perhaps the deceptive fragility.
They are light, diaphanous, but incredibly strong.

All the better for ripping off the ties that bind,
letting go, soaring free.

If a wise person were to see a woman with wings
they would not ask what these wings are for.

They would know.

* apologies to Paulo Coelho, *Veronika Decides to Die*

www.ingramcontent.com/pod-product-compliance
Lightning Source LLC
Chambersburg PA
CBHW070920080526
44589CB00013B/1385